LIFE IN LOCKDOWN: I CAUGHT THE K-FEVER

THE FIRST WAVE

by Three
세

© 2020 by Three

All rights reserved. No part of this book may be used or reproduced, distributed, or transmitted in any manner, including but not limited to, photocopying, recording, or other electronic or mechanical methods, without written permission from the author, except in the case of brief quotations embodied in critical articles or reviews.

Life in Lockdown: I Caught the K-Fever

ISBN 9798675818310

For more information, contact the author at angelabs@yahoo.com

Life in Lockdown: I Caught the K-Fever

The First Wave

For the one true "K."
My King.
Without Him,
I am nothing.

PROLOGUE   **The Onset**

Coronavirus 2019. Renamed COVID-19 later on.

The whole world never imagined waking up one day with a deadly pandemic that will shake everything up. COVID-19 is different from the previous ones. It is the real-life Thanos. In one snap, a person we know is either sick or had passed on. Everyone can feel there is something in the air, aside from the virus. Like Goblin's Grim Reaper prowling day and night, death is just walking in the streets and within one's neighborhood. It is an accurate picture the pandemic had painted in my mind.

Then quarantine happened. International lockdowns and border closures became inevitable as if each country was segregated by an invisible bubble. We learned to be self-sustaining: planting our food, baking our bread, trimming our hair, and entertaining our selves. The internet had been the only lifeline that connected us. Zoom became a household name that united networks separated either by a mile or by continents. Humans embraced all of this self-dependence rather than leaving their little protective shells of a home in the name of safety and public health. As social animals, they lived the solitary confinement imposed upon them so that they can live on and cope.

How about you? What kept you sane at that time?

It's the entertain-yourself part that got me going. Thanks to my Netflix and Viu subscriptions and to a dozen friends who had been suggesting Korean teledramas. I must admit that aside from praying, the shows had successfully taken the paranoia off my head. K-dramas came at a time when I needed a different kind of diversion, something I had not tried. A light form of escape to alleviate a heavy form of mental anguish that many had faced or are still facing.

This pandemic is this generation's ultimate scar. It has left an imprint that will forever change many lives. To some, it is a battle scar that needs to be healed and unseen. While for others, it is a pretty mark of endless learning and discoveries.

To me, it is when my incurable wanting for K-dramas has sprung.

CONTENTS

Dedication v
Prologue vi
Chapter 1: The Symptoms 1
Chapter 2: Catching the Fever 7
Chapter 3: The Strains 13
Chapter 4: The Side Effects 16
Chapter 5: The Infected 28
Chapter 6: My Specialist 42
Chapter 7: The Cure 49
Epilogue 66
Acknowledgments 70
Images of the Second Wave 73
Who is Three? 78
EXTRA!!! EXTRA!!! 81

x

CHAPTER 1

THE SYMPTOMS

I woke up like this: shocked that the world was engulfed with a highly contagious virus. However, I never imagined myself catching the Korean drama fever. Ever! Why would I want to watch anything with a language that is foreign to me?

But let me tell you about my pop culture orientation. As a Generation-X kid, my mother would allow me and my siblings to sit down in front of the boob tube that was tuned in to an English children's show. Our puppy dog eyes would look forward to that television time after our morning bath and dose of vitamins. My doting mom would give us our morning snacks while we watch TV to make us behave and give her some time for chores and personal stuff. This way, we picked up our English early on before we even went to school. Staples back then were *Fraggle Rock*, *New Zoo Revue*, *Felix the Cat*, *The Great Space Coaster*, and of course *Sesame Street*! I also remember following local shows such as *Uncle Bob's Lucky Seven Club*, *Batibot*, and *Kulit Bulilit*. I was also into animation such as *Voltes V*, *He-Man*, *Transformers*, *Pacman*, *Mighty Man and the Yukk*, *Looney Tunes*, *Woody Wood Pecker*, *Scooby-Doo*, etc. At five years old and for the first time, I went to the cinema and watched *Superman* with my aunts and uncles.

My father also made sure that as a family, we had TV time together at night. We were exposed early on to WWE matches, *Starsky and Hutch*, *Wonder Woman*, *Incredible Hulk*, *V*, *Rin-Tin-Tin*, *Knight Rider*, *Moonlighting*, and a host of other evening series popular at that time.

It's not obvious that I am a product of pop culture, right? Haha! Movies, music, series, and even TV commercials/jingles played inside my young mind, switching on and off as I was getting older. But it was more of our country's colonial past that the Western culture ingrained so much in us. I grew up listening to English songs that my dad played in his turntable. My siblings and I memorized many songs by The Beatles, Tom Jones, Engelbert Humperdinck, The Queen, Matt Monroe, and many others. I acquired this interest in pop music and movies because of this childhood habit. My late grandpa bought me a cassette tape, my first ever, of the Smokey Mountain, a teen pop group in the Philippines. Then I saw myself collecting tapes of some of my favorites such as New Kids on the Block, and Tommy Page!

Even as a pre-teen, I remember having my first crush on then child actor David Mendenhall who played Michael, the son of a trucker (Lincoln Hawk, played by Sylvester Stallone) in *Over the Top* (1987).

As an adult, I have watched multiple times all 10 seasons of *Friends*, was fascinated at *Supernatural*, drawn to *Santa Clarita Diet*, *To All the Boys I've Loved Before*, and a host of other TV series in my Netflix's My List. I ogled on Jimmy Fallon on *The Tonight Show* and went to the New York studio to watch live.

I can go on citing how Western pop culture shaped the way I am. On the contrary, I could not fully explain why I suddenly got hooked into this genre of K-pop culture. It must have been because I've exhausted all the English films and series I wanted to watch on Netflix. The need to fix my mind on something else during a pandemic was a non-negotiable for me.

The first symptom I remember having was the curiosity brought about by social media posts about this one immensely famous Korean drama series *사랑의 불시착* aka *Crash Landing on You*, or more popularly known as CLOY. I had no single idea who the actors were nor what the plot was. I was a stranger in the K-drama universe. One day, I read a post written by a respected government authority figure whom I was following on Facebook. He was recommending his followers to watch CLOY because "you are missing half of your life" (if you don't watch it). I got curious. So how come someone as dignified as him would endorse it? It must be that great. That was the last straw! I told myself that I should finally see it.

I did the first step. I turned on my Netflix. I saw it was number one in the most-watched list. Without expectations, I pressed the play button. Before I knew it, I was already in episode four the first time I watched. Followed by the late-night binge-watching and the on-the-road viewing using my mobile phone. (Signs of a hooked newbie, I know!) No, I didn't catch the fever! YET. It was just the first symptom. Hahaha!

I caught myself giddy in-between my binges. Not a great sign. I was magnetized! CLOY opened up a whole new world. (Cue: A Whole New World chorus) It is a world where I see Asian creativity and entertainment reflecting real life, light at the heart, and with all the feels. Two more K-dramas and hours and hours of screen time, it was when I knew I finally caught the K-fever.

CHAPTER 2

CATCHING THE FEVER

The secret of K-dramas' contagiousness and appeal is apparent. People watch novelty dramas to be entertained and steer away temporarily from their issues, self-inflicted and otherwise. So what factors endeared me to K-dramas?

Refreshing themes

Be they romantic comedy, horror, fantasy, or action, Korean series themes and scenes are often varied. I was enthused by the swapping of identities between the lovers in *Secret Garden* (*시크릿 가든*). Split personality disorders are not often tackled in a love story as it was done in *Hyde, Jekyll, Me* (*하이드, 지킬, 나*). Zombie plots always occur in modern days but *Kingdom*'s zombie apocalypse is in the

Joseon era. It's rare to find a love story that emerged from the DMZ, between a southerner and a northerner as depicted in *Crash Landing on You* (*사랑의 불시착*). Oh, and not to forget the computer game dimension intertwining with reality on *Memories of the Alhambra* (*알함브라 궁전의 추억*)!

Subtle portrayal

I noticed that K-dramas are not vulgar. I've gotten used to English flicks and series where the actors throw the "f"-word left and right. Sex, nakedness, and profanity are overrated in Hollywood movies. Meanwhile, K-dramas are subtle in portraying these, or most of the time, none of these at all. The delicate parts are always implied, not shown. I have not seen any scene where lovers or casual friends make love like in real life, in their naked glories. Kissing scenes are portrayed wholesomely, with a certain degree of innocence. Goes to show that indecency is not necessary for a movie or series to be a success.

Food and culture

Watching K-dramas takes me to South Korea. The lockdowns made the neighborhood a scary and unhealthy place. So K-dramas were the best form of travel I could have. I always look forward to dine-in scenes where the actors would indulge in *kimchi*, *ramyeon*, *tteokbokki*, *samgyetang*, *cha*, *soju*, *maegju*, etc. The "let's have lunch/dinner" culture is a glimpse of Korean amity. Food takes the centerpiece in any gathering. Karaoke night (*noraebang*) is a creative way to celebrate a milestone or for just an after-office get-together. K-dramas put a premium on good conversations that take place in coffee shops, restaurants, or even food stalls. The place they eat in is just as important as the company they keep.

Family values

Children honoring their *abeoji* (father), *omeoni* (mother), and an elderly person is a common trait of the characters in a K-drama. Family members look up to the dad as the head of the family and make the final decisions for family matters. Forgiveness and loyalty are of high value during conflicts. The families are conservative, making K-dramas stand out among its other Asian counterparts. There was a time when a string of Filipino drama movies and series highlighted storylines about troubles in the household brought about by mistress-wife squabbles or a philandering husband or wife. For brownie points from advertisers and patrons, heavy drama scenes with buckets of tears (and/or blood) bombarded these movies and series. This kind of storyline causes viewers' fatigue. However, in K-dramas, family values are upheld over emotional roller-coasters. The quiet resolve that the K-drama characters have exudes honor and dignity.

New words

The most entertaining way to learn Hangeul is by watching K-dramas. Going beyond *saranghae*, *gamsahabnida*, *annyeong*, *ne*, *ani-o*, and *oppa*, I decided to study basic Korean. The Seoul-based language teacher I met through a common friend has been mentoring me. She wrote some thoughts about K-dramas in one of the chapters. I hope to learn Korean further as I indulge in more K-dramas.

Feel-good vibes

It never fails. Watching K-dramas somehow releases any mental, emotional, and physical stress. Maybe it is the story, the acting, the setting, the soundtrack, or the total package itself. It has become my end-of-day treat. Nighttime is an exciting time as I get to cozy up on the couch while watching episodes of my latest fixation.

CHAPTER 3

THE STRAINS

On my video-on-demand list are:
- *Crash Landing On You*
- *Itaewon Class*
- *What's Wrong with Secretary Kim?*
- *Secret Garden*
- *Hyde, Jekyll, Me*
- *Kingdom (seasons I and II)*
- *She was Pretty*
- *Fight for My Way*
- *Memories of the Alhambra*
- *Something in the Rain*
- *Revolutionary Love*
- *Mystic Pop-up Bar*
- *Reply 1988*
- *Goblin (Guardian: The Lonely and Great God)*
- *My Fellow Citizens*
- *Touch Your Heart*

It's Okay to Not be Okay
Hwarang

(As of press time, this list has yet to be updated.)

In the commentary part, I handpicked only a few from the list so as not to make a novel out of this book. I may have favored the series starring Hyun Bin, Park Seo Joon, Choi Siwon, and Lee Dong Wook. As a newbie, naturally, I started my K-drama walk by watching familiar (handsome) faces first. The *oppa*, as they say. Haha! Although no doubt that acting-wise, these men are "it." The storylines were all great, too.

To those who are planning to begin their K-drama journey, you'll notice some commonalities: Subway - which seems to be the official K-drama sandwich *sigdang* (restaurant), and the three "Fs:" fighting, food, and flashbacks.

"Fighting!" You'll hear the characters exclaim this from time to time. It is to encourage someone to pursue a goal. It's like saying that one should not surrender and keep it up.

Food. Well, just thinking about the coffee shops, food stalls, pubs, and restaurant scenes makes me hungry. Korean dishes play a major part in each series; a very effective way to promote tourism and culture.

Flashbacks never go out of style. Instead of a character explaining situations and ordeals in words, viewers would be taken to occasional flashbacks. These flashbacks appear sporadically and complete the puzzle. If you put them together, you will be surprised at the big reveal.

Enjoy!!!

CHAPTER 4

THE SIDE EFFECTS

Am I the only one who watches K-dramas and gets attracted to the food shown in the episodes? Sudden cravings have now found their way to my daily life. Helpful K-friends satisfy this fixation for K-food. One sells kimchi to me. Another suggests noodle brands and sends me recipes and photos of other dishes to try. The good thing is, Korean food is not so hard to find. Many businesses offering K-goods have been flourishing since the ongoing wave of K-fanbase began. It seems the K-phenomenon is here to stay.

I've also mentioned that I've been learning Hangeul online. I met my gracious Seoul-based teacher through our common friend--- I teach her English while she teaches me Korean. The fab thing is, we do not only talk about languages but every session is like a cultural exchange. I tell her about life in my motherland and my life in a new country. She, in turn, tells me what it is like living in South Korea. We talk about writers, authors, books, movies, TV series, actors/actresses, and of course, food!

How about you? What are the side effects that came along with this obsession with K-dramas? As for me, read on.

*****

Even before being a K-drama fan, I have been an avid kimchi consumer. My preference for this spicy fermented dish seems to have been doubly ignited as I feasted my eyes on the characters indulging in it. My friend whose business is selling their family's grandma-style kimchi has become my regular supplier to satisfy my kimchi cravings.

(The brand! Who wouldn't buy, yes?)

*****

Aside from being a side dish, I use kimchi to make kimchi fried rice.

Here's a simple recipe. In a non-stick wok, stir mashed left-over cooked rice. Add diced chicken sausage and a few drops of olive oil. Continue stirring for three minutes in medium heat. Add kimchi. Stir for another three to five minutes until the rice mixture is even with kimchi sauce. Top each serving with a sunny-side-up egg.

*****

Hours before the lockdown was declared, I had an afternoon snack at this Korean tea place and tried the gynostemma tea which is said to lower blood pressure and has anti-obesity properties. Sign of aging. ☺

*****

I make my mandu (Korean dumpling). The recipe is simple. Chop leeks and spinach finely to make two cups. In a bowl, combine 300 grams of minced chicken, leeks, spinach, and two teaspoons of black pepper. Make sure that the ingredients are well incorporated.

Scoop out one tablespoon and place it on a round dumpling wrapper. Fold the wrapper in two. Seal by lightly wetting and pressing between the folds. Steam, pan- or deep-fry. Quick and easy for snacking or viand. Tip: Use soy sauce with lemon or calamansi as a dip.

*****

On one special occasion, I made a *dosirak* (like a Japanese *bento*) with Korean chicken pops, my mandu, kimchi, and a fried egg on top of rice.

This one is also easy. To make the mandu, just follow my recipe. For the chicken pops, I bought a Korean-branded one and fried it according to package instructions. For the egg, cook according to your preference. Have a serving of steamed or fried rice. It's up to you to make the plating fancy or not. Don't forget your kimchi!

*****

The next photo is my couscous kimbap. This is a bit complicated to do. But if you keep doing it, you'd be happy with the outcome. Here's how:

First, make sticky couscous by simmering the grains with more water. Turn off the heat when they look well-done and moist. Set it aside and let it cool down for a few minutes.

Second, slice crabsticks thinly. Set aside.

Open a canned tuna flakes and set aside.

Place a seaweed sheet, with the shiny side facing up, on top of a bamboo rolling mat. When the couscous is ready, scoop a portion. Gently flatten and spread on ¾ of the wrap.

Next, place crabsticks horizontally following the direction of the roll.

Then top the spread with tuna flakes, lightly press. Make sure not to overcrowd.

Now you are ready to roll. Carefully make a small fold starting from the side of the bamboo mat that is nearest to you and slightly press on the seaweed wrap. From that position, slightly lift the bamboo mat, and make that first roll. Slightly press. Slowly continue this rolling-and-pressing cycle until you reach the end.

Tip: Always press firmly but lightly. Sticky couscous and a filling that is not overcrowded make a good roll.

To slice, use a thin-edge knife if you don't have a sushi knife. This is to ensure smooth cutting. Another tip: Lightly wet the knife with water before slicing.

*****

Kimchijeon (kimchi pancake), another delicious kimchi dish, is my latest favorite. The ingredients are scallion, 2 cups kimchi, cooking oil, 1 cup all-purpose flour, ¼ cup cornstarch, 1 egg, and 1 cup icy cold water.

Instructions: Thinly slice the kimchi and the scallion. Combine flour, cornstarch, kimchi sauce, egg, and water in a bowl. Stir lightly, do not overmix. Add a bit more water if the batter becomes thick. Add in kimchi and scallion to the batter. Mix gently. In a pan, heat a tablespoon of oil. Pour a scoop of batter and spread on the pan evenly to form a round shape. Turn it over when the edges become brown and crispy.

Optional: Minced chicken may be added but must be fried first before adding to the batter with the scallions and kimchi. To make a dip, combine a tablespoon of soy sauce, a teaspoon of vinegar, a tablespoon of water, half teaspoon sugar, and a pinch of black pepper.

*****

These next photos are some of my Korean writing exercises. My teacher likes my penmanship. I hope to hear her also say that I am already fluent. Wishful thinking! Hangeul reading is not hard. But the writing/spelling is a bit confusing because of some vowel sounds. I also have to memorize hundreds of new words.

Studying a new language is not new to me. I took up some Spanish in college and studied French a few years ago. Hangeul does not have words that are similar or close to similar in English. Some Spanish and French words are derivatives of English that's why they're easier to learn.

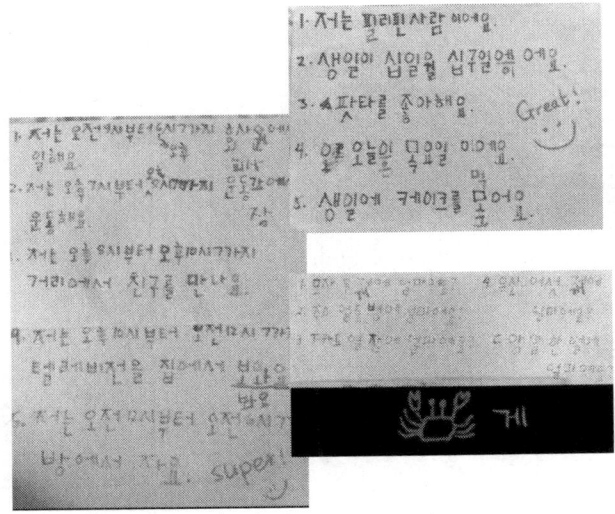

"Crab" (ge) is not the same as "piece"(gae).

CHAPTER 5

THE INFECTED

I know a lot of people who got infected by this fever as well. It's been going on even before the pandemic.

Janet del Rosario, a housewife from Malaysia

"K-dramas are very relatable. They show a lot of the good side of life without making it too fairytale-like. They teach a lot about friendships, family, love, sacrifices, struggles, and victories. And interposed in all these is the right amount of humor that balances off the tear-jerking and vulnerable

scenes and that makes the characters endearing, alive, and real. On top of that, the actors play their roles very well in almost all of the k-dramas I watched. The onscreen chemistry of the lead actors is really good and when they play tender scenes together, they can tug at any viewer's heartstrings.

"My favorites are:

- *Reply 1988 - This series resonates well with me. I related a lot in many of the scenes shown in this series. This captured the fun, the brevity of life during the '80s. It showed very realistic situations at home - dealing with day to day struggles among siblings, between husband and wife, friends, and even people in the neighborhood. This is a series that is very close to home and evoked a lot of good memories and emotions in me.*

- *It's Okay that's Love - This series is about the stigma of having mental health issues. It is very informative and showed a good picture of how people with mental illnesses struggle and how important it is for those around them to continue to love them and care for them and not write them off in their lives as hopeless individuals. This is mind-opening to those who are mentally healthy and on the other hand, give hope to those who are suffering from any form of mental illness.*
- *Crash Landing on You - Beyond the beautiful love story, the central theme of this drama is that at the core of every Korean (whether from North or South) is a human soul that knows how to care, love, respect and value life and is willing to sacrifice for the ones they love. I love how this drama*

humanizes the North Koreans, though this may not be taken well by them. Additionally, I like Yoon Seri's quote "Sometimes the wrong train takes you in the right direction". To me it simply means that nothing in life happens by chance, things always happen for a reason.

"I have watched a lot of K-dramas and the storylines are varied - fantasy, drama, comedy, action, family-oriented, and so on. I am not sure if there is any storyline that has yet to be made into a K-drama. And probably that is the reason why K-dramas are so popular, you can watch stories from any genre. I would just really want to watch more romcoms - preferably with Hyun Bin and Son Hye Jin as main leads (wink).

"Hyun Bin (CLOY), Son Hye Jin (CLOY and Personal Taste), Lee Min Ho (City Hunter), Ji Chang Wook (Healer), Kim Soo

Hyun (*My Love from the Stars, it's okay to not be okay*) and Park Bo Young (*Strong Girl Bong Soon* and *Abyss*) are all great actors. Beyond their pretty faces are great acting skills. Aja, fighting!"

*****

Rona Hernandez, a Human Resource practitioner from the Philippines

"*I love K-drama storyline + the characters + setting. My favorite is Goblin, Weightlifting Fairy Kimbo-Joo, Doctor Crush, Sky Castle, and Reply 1988 because of their storyline and the characters.*"

*****

Junne Grajales, a communications professional from the Philippines

"*I like K-dramas because of its clever approach in addressing sensitive matters (mental health, infidelity, and breaking away from tradition), quality productions (cinematography +*

costume designs), and mind-blowing plot twists.

"My favorites are:

- *Reply 1988 - funny without trying too hard, no antagonist (the conflict is within you), a great portrayal of family life and genuine friendship in the '80s, brilliant and authentic enough '80s set design, I like that it also featured a strong story arc for the adult roles, all the actors carried each other and genuinely portrayed their characters, and lotsa relatable life lessons (middle child syndrome, menopause, and money issues, etc.)!*
- *Goblin - made me cry a lot (love is more powerful than death) + terrific comedic timing, good cast camaraderie, wonderful*

costume designs for the male stars, raw depiction of sibling love, fresh perspective on the loss of life and reincarnation, beautiful story progression, and incredible plot twist

- *Weightlifting Fairy Kim Bok Joo - heartwarming, hilarious take on dating life, magnificent acting for lead star Lee Sung Kyung, a different slant on gender issues (female weightlifter, eats a lot, kissed the boy first, etc.), and stellar chemistry between the two lead actors.*

"K-Dramas have already represented several storylines that have piqued my interest---deeper dive into relationships (Go Back Couple and Because This Is My First Life), reincarnation (Chicago Typewriter and Mystic Pop-Up Bar), and mind-altering stories

(The King: Eternal Monarch and Memorist). I could not ask for more hehe.

"For Won Bin haha: I hope you do a TV series again soon! ☺"

*****

Adrian Ayalin, a journalist from the Philippines

"K-dramas are entertaining, (and) relaxing, especially romantic comedies. Their use of flashbacks is also very effective. I like CLOY, Something in the Rain, and What's Wrong with Secretary Kim? (I want to see) More stories involving North Korean characters.

"My message for Son Ye Jin and Park Seo Joon: You rock! Hope to meet you someday. Lol."

*****

Joy Sadie-Bush, an office administrator from the U.S.

"The stories are so not Hollywood. I love When Camellia Blooms - It hit home since the main character is a single mom (I was, for a long time). The actors portrayed their characters well. The storyline does not bore- there is a love story, mystery, family, and community dynamics. I am currently watching Misaeng and I'm truly loving the acting and writing on this one. I am pretty sure there are tons of K-dramas out there that I would love the storyline because they are just that competitive. I just hope they don't stop writing creative storylines.

"Kang Haneul, you the best! And a shout-out to the child star Kang Hoon. He is my favorite Korean actor ☺."

*****

Ruby Mercado, a housewife from the Philippines

"(I love K-dramas because) they're very light-hearted and decent to watch. My favorite is CLOY, because of the acting, the cast, and the love story. I would like to see more action in the storylines."

*****

Gener del Mundo, a head of Creatives from the Philippines

"What I love most about K-Dramas is the originality of their storylines. The main plots are great to watch but the subplots will keep you excited as well. I also enjoy seeing the Korean way of life through these series. I like to learn about their cultures and traditions and I love sceneries/locations.

"(My favorite series is) Reply 1988. Somehow, the story and characters are very *relatable to us Filipinos. There is parallelism here that's very Pinoy yet it's Korean. The actors were really good. The production design is fantastic because it was produced in 2015 but the setting is 1988. Technically, it's almost a period movie. It was a long series but there wasn't a dull moment in any episode."*

*****

Tin Torres, a Human Resource specialist from the Philippines

"What I love most about K-dramas is the storyline. My favorite series is Goblin because I love the storyline/script, the cinematography is superb, the official soundtrack is awesome, and the actors are great."

*****

Malou Claudio, an entrepreneur from the Philippines

"K-dramas have a wide range of varieties from melodrama, rom-com, thriller, and

are well-made. I want to see more heroism stories such as Disney's Mulan.

"My message to my favorite actor Ji Chang Wook: Sleep with me, please. Hahaha!"

*****

Marian Cabahug, a music teacher from the Philippines

"I love K-dramas because of the creative way they make the funny scenes and because of the storylines that usually have a glimpse of their positive cultural practices.

"(My favorites are) Moon Lovers and Legend of the Blue Sea··· (They are) super funny."

*****

Michelle Cruz-Chua, a lifestyle and well-being coordinator from Australia

"I am just a beginner with regards to K-dramas. I just watched two dramas but what strikes me most are the nice places seen in the episodes that I can't wait to travel to Korea. The storyline is creative and fresh that brings out from the viewers' hearts. Not to mention the good looking actors that make me 'kilig' (giddy). You will see the attractiveness of all people in them.

"Since I only watched two K-dramas (for now), I like What's Wrong with Secretary Kim? because it's a happy-to-watch romantic comedy series. How amazingly well this drama is filmed as a whole. The scenes work well together and the cohesiveness of the entire

cast is amazing. I think that because the main characters have such a high level of chemistry between them, it makes the drama seem so realistic, instead of feeling like it is fake. There is always romance and comedy intertwined with each other."

*****

CHAPTER 6

MY SPECIALIST

It's been a privilege to include in my first book my Hangeul teacher and friend, Kate. I mentioned earlier that it is not just language talk but also of cultural exchange every time we talk online. I asked her if she can write her thoughts about some of my questions on K-drama, and she willingly obliged. Here are her answers to a curious learner's (aka me) questions about Korean drama.

Me: As a Korean, what can you say about millions of people loving K-pop?

Kate: *K-pop didn't get popular in an instant. Many causes fit and spread through YouTube.*

Not everyone can be a singer in Korea. I don't know if this is good or not, but it seems to be working well with capitalism. The young who pass auditions at a large agency spend a long time as trainees practicing dancing and singing. The agency also makes songs through thorough planning. Only groups that are perfectly prepared in everything have a chance to be on stage. I read an article that BTS only practiced until the choreography was perfectly synchronized. Through thorough market analysis, they make songs that would be good for listeners around the world. Among the group members are people from other countries. Because language is necessary to communicate with fans. Auditions are coming from all over the world and global producers are participating to create an idol group. It may be a natural result for fans around the world to fall into an idol group that shows perfect performance.

Me: Do you believe that the K-drama phenomenon has an end or you think it will stay for a very long time?

Kate: *It's likely to last for a while before something new comes out. With this 'Parasite' movie or 'Kingdom,' it seems that many people are getting more interested in Korean content.*

Me: What are your K-drama favorites and why do you like them?

Kate: *Mr. Sunshine---we had a hard time facing straight at the Japanese occupation period. But through this drama, I felt thankful I did not face that era. It was told to me that many people silently fought and died in their positions for our independence. Reply 1998--- perhaps the memories of our parents' generation were poverty and hunger caused by war. We may be the first generation to recall happy childhood memories. It is a drama that warms the emotional heart of the era with affection between neighbors and friends. Itaewon Class---it reflects the times these days and gives dreams and hopes to young people.*

Me: Is it true that when a girl invites a guy for *ramyeon*, it means that the girl is tempting the guy to do something privately?

Kate: *In One Fine Spring Day (봄날은 간다), the heroine Lee Young-ae tells the man who drove her to the front of her house, 'Do you want some ramen?' ('라면 먹을래요?') After that, their love begins. Because of this scene, the sentence seems to have begun to imply otherwise. 'Do you want some ramen?' ('라면 먹을래요?') simply indirectly expresses permission to come into one's house.*

Me: Why do you think that sex and vulgarity are not emphasized and are not common subjects in K-dramas?

Kate: *Personally, aren't you watching dramas to be happy? A glimpse of such a similar situation will allow the viewers to unfold their imagination. Leaving a chance to imagine rather than showing it all could make the drama richer. If you want an R-rated drama, you can watch something else. There are various channels. You can easily access the K-contents with English subtitles.*

Me: What is the edge of K-dramas over all the other Asian and Western series?

Kate: *There was a time when I was into American dramas for a while. As the season progressed without ending, I felt that the drama I enjoyed was a repetition of the pattern. Korean dramas usually consist of 16-20 episodes and have a definite ending. Also, there are various materials and genres. Korean dramas are clean. Not violent or sexual. I've read an article about American mothers who want their children to listen to K-pop instead of pop. This is because there is no bad content and positive lyrics have a good effect on children just like Love Yourself of BTS. Additionally, there are attractive actors. They are good looking and well-dressed. Wouldn't it satisfy our inherent desires? Doesn't a handsome man (make you) feel good just by looking at him? :-)*

Me: Do you also like pork rind and soju? I always see these enjoyed by the characters in many scenes. Hehe⋯

Kate: *No, I don't like it. I like pork belly (삼겹살) and beer.*

Me: Why do people singing in karaoke nights use tambourines?

Kate: *Norae-Bang (노래방) is a place to relieve stress by singing passionately with friends or colleagues. Although it is changing now, this is a company dining culture. The intention is to get closer and communicate with colleagues and juniors who work together by drinking. The tambourine is intended to create such an atmosphere of entertainment.*

This curious student had asked so many other questions. I suddenly wanted to grab a few shots of soju. But I'm reserving that in our actual *seonsaengnim-hagsaeng* (teacher-student) one-for-the-road.

CHAPTER 7

THE CURE

I pray every day. I read my Bible. I gain peace by practicing these habits, no doubt. And my gain from catching the K-fever? My answer is simple: It's a personal cure, acting as a filter of chaotic news.

K-drama-viewing brings a reprieve from the daily news about COVID-19, the political divide arising from the pandemic, the statistics on people plunged in poverty because of business shutdowns, etc. These are soul-arresting events.

Albeit temporary, the satisfaction I get from these K-stories is notable. We get to talk and think about something else, not about the current crisis, not about suffering while waiting for the vaccine.

Don't get me wrong. I'm not saying one should spend all day watching the dramas nor sleep in the wee hours after binge-watching. I still get to finish other important matters. Important matters = daily chores, working online, blogging, working out, learning Hangeul, and writing this book. It's not all TV and internet for me. I bake different kinds of chocolate cake, brownie, and bread recipes. The family play card games and Monopoly. I do other things. It's all about time management and discipline.

K-dramas are not just plain entertainment avenues. The stories have nuggets of wisdom and truth.

For purposes of not spoiling the plot of the shows listed in Chapter 3, I only wrote about my viewing take-aways and purposely selected only a few of my favorites. If you're looking for a thorough critique, you won't see it in my writing. Google is the answer if you are after professional reviews of the dramas.

*****

Take, for instance, *Crash Landing on You*. Never have I encountered such a plot. We've seen star-crossed lovers but not one that blossomed from the critical border of the two Koreas. At least not in my viewing experience, so far.

This story asks the question that if love does not conquer all, then what will? I like the fact that the two stayed with each other, realizing along the way that they were in love. Imagine if Capt. Ri (played by Hyun Bin) would just throw Se-ri (portrayed by Son Ye-jin) under the bus, or if he'd just think of his career and safety instead of the welfare of this person who was in a predicament. It won't be an easy decision for any ordinary man as it was not also easy for a brave army officer like Capt. Ri. But he saved her anyway in the name of love! The story progressed on a rough ride that I was hooked until the climax. It is an adventurous love story.

>>RECOMMENDED FOR great acting, cultural values, morals, unique plot
>>LOOK FORWARD TO the chemistry between Hyun Bin and Son Yejin, the sites in Switzerland, the charm of Hyun Bin

*****

Itaewon Class may seem idealistic, yes. But the perseverance and fervor in Park Saeroyi (played by Park Seo-joon) was something worth emulating. The madman of a villain went to all extent just to make Saeroyi miserable; and yet our protagonist remained steadfast. Saeroyi was inspiring. He demonstrated that to pursue one's greatest goal, the drive must remain even if the obstacles seem insurmountable. However, I won't use revenge as a driving force to attain something. It could be an effective push but it is a stressful and bitter means. I may want to have to unload all the baggage first before I can move forward.

If there's one shallow thing I'd change, that would be Park Seo-joon's hairstyle throughout the program! Haha! It's the opposite of his cool hairstyles in his other series.

>>RECOMMENDED FOR pep talk and motivation, values on family, friendship, work ethics, and loyalty
>>LOOK FORWARD TO the love triangle (who Saeroyi chose), the gender and racial issues

*****

Park Seo-joon and Hwang Jung-eum played the main characters in the romantic comedy *She Was Pretty*. This story of a lingering young love would enthrall viewers. It began when a boy and a girl looked out for each other. As they matured, their friendship grew deeper. Both of them knew they wanted to formalize this relationship. But the conflicts arose when the girl felt inferior because she did not grow up to be as pretty and as an achiever as when they were still kids. The rest of the story revolved around how the now grown-up woman manifested this insecurity by disguising. You should watch how the rest of the story unfolds.

I used to think that the love I felt when I was younger would be the same even as the years went by. I also used to think that love was only about feelings. For a time, I was that person who believed that friendship is always the best foundation before becoming lovers. God writes our love stories and it is up to us to act on the choices or not. This one is about a persistent love that cannot separate two people. No distance, no time, or even fading beauty can come in between them.

This series also depicted potential conflicts in a relationship such as a new person coming in between and offers unreciprocated love, the kind that knows no condition. There was even a moment when I was rooting for Choi Siwon's character, being this new guy whose love for the main lady character was unrequited. Their love triangle was like an '80s love song that pops the make-or-break question: Are you going to choose the one who loves you or the one you love? (Cue: the late Glenn Frey, sorry millennials.)

\>\>RECOMMENDED FOR sweetness factor (hehe), great acting, moral and friendship values, some marketing/advertising career touchpoints
\>\>LOOK FORWARD TO the chemistry between the lead actors, the charisma of Park Seojoon and Choi Siwon, the love triangle (who the lady chose), dining scenes

*****

The love that you've been looking for has been in front of you for the longest time and you just did not notice. That's the main message and charm of *What's Wrong with Secretary Kim?*

Sometimes, this happens when two people who are overly familiar with each other did not imagine that a real non-platonic relationship between them is a possibility. The small attempts to deny the reality of a blooming love became small acts of affirmation that indeed, the unthinkable is happening. I think this conflict occurs too often in an office setting made complicated if it is between a boss and a subordinate.

The main characters (played by *ehem* Park Seo-joon---again, I know--- and Park Min-young) simplified it and acted upon what they think is right for the two of them. The excitement in the story develops every time the two tried hiding and suppressing their feelings for each other. When they became an item, they tried even harder to keep their affection from being noticed by the people around them.

The fun did not stop when everybody found out about their relationship.

>>RECOMMENDED FOR family and friendship values, work ethics, sweetness value (haha!)
>>LOOK FORWARD TO the chemistry between the lead actors, the funny romantic scenes, the dining scenes

*****

Would you get into a relationship with your best bud's older sister who happens to be your older sister's best friend? Do you consider it a taboo? *Something in the Rain* smoothly tackled the age gap issue as well as that invisible line of romance that friends should not dare cross, especially if the friendship is like familial.

Like me, a believer in friendship as the best origin of a non-platonic relationship, I think it is sweet to have a great friend since childhood and ending up with that person. No pretensions. No hidden past. Just the old version of the young you. I used to imagine a life like that. Having someone close by and share secrets with and eventually noticing how you two have grown to be the same people only in adult bodies.

Chances are, the parents and/or siblings would agree to this set-up since there is familiarity. But what if they don't and the conflict stems from the inner circle. That would be the hardest to deal with because instead of having no pretensions, you will do the opposite. You'll keep hiding until eventually everybody feels betrayed.

I'd do what the main characters did. Love is sweeter if shared with someone you know so well than with someone who does not know you deeply.

Son Yejin played the role of a lady who found real love in a younger man played by Jung Hae-in. Their chemistry was undeniable.

>>RECOMMENDED FOR family, friendship, and work values

>>LOOK FORWARD TO the chemistry between the lead actors, the restaurant scenes, the official soundtrack (surprised to hear *Save the Last Dance for Me*, a Bruce Willis old favorite in my playlist)

*****

We're all uniquely twisted one way or another. Some are accepting of it. Others are in denial. *It's Okay to Not be Okay* is not only about the complexities of man's psychological make-up. The intensity of the story's conflict overshadowed its simple theme of accepting one's ugly past, being free from it, and welcoming an uncertain future. The occasional graphic novel storytelling was an added attraction.

The writer successfully managed to make the viewers wonder who the real villain is. Again, for the reason that I don't want to be the best spoiler awardee, I'll not go farther. I'd limit my comments by saying that it takes a very discerning individual to know who to trust. If you have trust issues, that's alright. If you're gullible, that is alright, too. The drama shows the human faces of these extremes. We can learn so much from it.

Additionally, it underscores the idea that we have the power to choose for ourselves who we want to be part of our own family, blood-related or otherwise. One may have been born to a dysfunctional family, but a future one based on our ideals is possible.

>>RECOMMENDED FOR the outstanding acting by Oh Jung-se as the autistic brother, creative storytelling, unique plot and surprising reveals, friendship and family values

\>\>LOOK FORWARD TO the catchy songs, the graphics, the funny scenes, openness to people with special needs, attitudes towards mental illness, the chic attires of Seo Ye-Ji (the leading lady), the smiles of Soo Hyun (the lead actor)

*****

Do not mind the obvious age gap between the two lead stars of *Goblin*, otherwise known as *Guardian: The Lonely and Great God* (쓸쓸하고 찬란하神-도깨비). It is part of the plot whereby an immortal warrior is to be reunited with his destined bride in different periods in a lifetime.

Gong Yoo, who played the loyal Goryeo era soldier, effectively acted out the role of an expression-less but soft-hearted army leader. His journey into the modern world to meet his bride (played by Kim Go-Eun) will be the centerpiece of the story. It was a mix of romantic, funny, and thought-provoking scenes. One may wonder how a high schooler would be a bride to someone who has been in the world for 900 years. Find out how the contrasting characters of the bride (immature, playful, and spontaneous) and the immortal soldier (serious, reflecting, and unemotional) produce a love tale that transcends time and even continental boundaries. They magically travel wherever they want to go!

This modern-day fantasy will make viewers think about death and regrets. Loving someone, expressing that love, and choosing him/her above all things make life worth living. This part is made exciting by a charming Grim Reaper portrayed by Lee Dong Wook. His regrets for failing to choose his love interest (Sunny, played by Yoo In-Na) haunted him as he traversed his reincarnated life. They'd meet in the modern world as ill-fated lovers.

The parts played by Grim Reaper and Sunny in the tale of the immortal soldier and his bride revealed their intertwined past lives. This makes for an exciting backdrop. The charismatic characters played the parts so well.

>>RECOMMENDED FOR great acting, cultural, family, and friendship values, unique plot, beautiful location shots
>>LOOK FORWARD TO the chemistry between Lee Dong Wook and Yoo In-Na, the enigmatic charm of Lee Dong Wook, the fashionable Yoo In-Na

*****

I'm enamored by Lee Dong Wook. When I learned he hosts *Because I Want to*

Talk, I quickly turned on Viu and saw his pilot episode with Gong Yoo.

Moreover, after finishing *Goblin*, I watched *Touch Your Heart*. In the beginning, I thought it was a spin-off of the former. He teamed up once again with Yoo In-Na to play the same characters showed in the cliffhanger of *Goblin* in their supposedly reincarnated lives. I was wrong. It's a stand-alone romantic comedy with its sweet plot.

The series takes the viewers to an actress's colorful world and a lawyer's boxed life. With unpleasant first impressions, how love developed between two colleagues out of kindness and simplicity of spirit is how the story goes. Hence the title. It's an honest-to-goodness romantic comedy that satisfies anyone not looking for heavy melodramatic scenes. I enjoyed its straightforward approach towards finding love in the workplace, how co-workers could also develop affection for each other, and overcome conflicts that face them.

The viewers are also taken to a world of lawyers and prosecutors, courtroom drama, and lawyer-client relationship. Despite these, it managed not to become boring, and melded well with the lightness of the love story.

>>RECOMMENDED FOR work and friendship values, a look at legal proceedings, interesting plot
>>LOOK FORWARD TO the chemistry between Yoo In-Na and Lee Dong Wook, the stars' pretty attires, Lee Dong Wook's acting

EPILOGUE

We have entered into a different kind of war; a war against an enemy whose deadly weapons are unseen. It is not the same war that those who came before us faced. Our generation will never forget this time. The world has gone through many changes in a matter of three months or so. As of this writing, these changes, or what we call the "new normal," continues.

New things and words have emerged, some re-introduced:

- Dalgona coffee
- Basque burnt cheesecake
- Zoom call
- Social distancing
- TikTok
- WFH (work-from-home)
- Mask (surgical, washable, or N95)
- Alcohol
- Sanitizer
- Disinfectant
- Vitamin C, D, and Zinc
- Food deliveries
- Frontliner

- Lockdown
- Quarantine
- Covidiot
- BLM (Black Lives Matter)
- Maskne (acne due to mask-wearing)
- Coronavirus aka COVID-19 (word of the century!)

Like everyone else, I also have changed. This piece proves it. Never have I imagined that it would take a virus for me to finally write my first book. It was a goal after I graduated from university. I have volumes of poems and short stories kept in a box back in my home country. I even dreamed of owning a bookstore someday. I also never thought that instead of poetry and short stories, I'd be writing about a pandemic.

Let this work remind us of this season. It magnifies the harsh realities and the chasm that separates humans from each other: the rich versus the poor, the powerful versus the powerless, the strong versus the weak, the old versus the young, colored races versus the white, and some more in the spectrum of issues. This pandemic is the penultimate equalizer because death still reigns as the ultimate. Survival is still uncertain regardless of one's pedigree. Even the royals and state leaders were infected!

On a lighter note, this book reminds us to find our light on a dark path for the sake of sanity. I'd been spending quality time with family even before this happened. When the lockdowns began, I treasured the time with them even more. I was thinking that tomorrow is no guarantee. We played card games, we talked about things and people (hehe), and of course, we've maxed our Netflix subscription.

What kept you preoccupied?

As for me, when the lockdowns came, the K-drama floodgates opened and I was in front of it enjoying the swim and saying in Korean: "*gwaenchanh-ayo!*" (It's alright. No worries.) God is in control. Always.

ACKNOWLEDGMENTS

Gamsahabnida to:

- ❖ Kate Chang: My only Hangeul connection. Thanks to you, my seonsaengnim. I owe you big time.
- ❖ Gladys Figueroa: My link to Kate. TYVM.
- ❖ Lia Ocampo: For the encouragement. Visit authorlia.com. (Haha, a free ad!)
- ❖ Vanessa Velasco: For agreeing to be my editor. You're the best!
- ❖ Netflix and Viu: For providing entertainment in an insane world and time.
- ❖ Korean actors, producers, and those behind the K-drama novelty: Without

your wonderful works of art, life would be a tad boring. You've helped many people remain sane by providing quality entertainment during the lockdown.

- ❖ The testimonial senders (Adrian, Michelle, Marian, Malou, Ruby, Joy, Gener, Junne, Tin, Rona, and Janet): For your thoughts and appreciation for K-dramas representing the millions out there. Thanks for being their voice through my humble literary work.
- ❖ The Korean Tourism Organization: For access to the KL headquarters.
- ❖ The governments: For the declaration of lockdowns. If not for those, many more would have succumbed, physically or mentally. I wouldn't have looked at K-dramas in a new light.

- ❖ My prayer warriors: For cheering me on.
- ❖ My parents: For a simple life made enjoyable by a childhood of pop culture.
- ❖ My family: For making the lockdown bearable. Thankful for the clever opinions and for tolerating this new fixation of mine. Above all, know that you guys are my most treasured people on earth! Saranghaeyo!
- ❖ My Father: For being the best source of things seen and unseen. Words are insufficient for what my heart wants to say.

IMAGES OF THE SECOND WAVE

| 74

Wouldn't it be nice? Hint, hint…

Just scan the QR code for the Gangwon Tour app.

Information from the Korean Tourism Organization.

| 75

And when the bell tolls,
it's time to taste and see them all…

77

WHO IS THREE?

The better question is "Why 'Three'?"

Three was inspired by Ten (played by Choi Siwon), the character from She was Pretty, an author hiding in that pseudonym. Ten is overflowing with unconditional love, embodying the kind that is almost humanly impossible.

Three lives away from her motherland. She wants to keep traveling until she is too old to do it. Maybe writing, too.

Three believes that nothing is too significant that it will stay forever. Nothing is too unimportant that it will not have a purpose or function.

Three does not go after fame or fortune. Like everything else, these things will also pass.

Three wants to remain anonymous for she is just a small dot in a vast universe from the very start.

Three thinks that the world does not revolve around her because she is not the sun. Hence this useless uninformative bio that you are reading right now. Haha!

Until the second wave, *salamdeul*! By then, it's more about the place where the K-fever originated. It's going to be about life after lockdown...

EXTRA!!! EXTRA!!!

One of my diversions during the lockdown was writing. I came up with a short series of social media posts called "Quarantips." It's about some things, practically amusing and otherwise, that one can do to save resources while being held at home.

- Save electricity. Especially now that everyone is using power at home. So stop opening that fridge too often! Take your mind off that food! 😁
- Don't waste precious time. Continue exercising your brain cells. That's why I'm now on my second week seriously studying Hangul (Korean) with a certified Seoul-based teacher. I need to prepare for that encounter with Hyun Bin. 😁😁
- Don't shop online for clothes, bags, and shoes. They can wait. You still can't use them for now, anyway. Food first. Function before fashion.

- Try to use up to only three ingredients max when cooking. In short, don't cook with complicated recipes to save on supply. Use spices instead. I usually cook with complete ingredients but a little sacrifice won't hurt in times like this. Be creative. Boil. Do not fry that egg. Saves you oil and salt. 😄
- To those who want fairer skin, now is your time (to shine)! No need to get glutathione dose or whitening lotion as staying indoors for a long time will do the trick. All you need is vitamin D. So try to get some sun on your patio for a few minutes. ☺
- This is the time to clean inboxes and delete hundreds of useless emails to save on gigabytes. So ditch those antiquated love letters. Don't hang on. 😊 Save your emotions. Being emotionally and mentally healthy is important these days. ☺

Would you like to have a published article on a travel website for free? Be a contributor and send that travel article to inspire other travelers and voyagers-to-be. For more info, visit

The Travel Peoples.com

You may also check
https://facebook.com/thetrvlppls

Made in the USA
Columbia, SC
30 January 2022